GOD'S PRECIOUS Promises

Gary C. Wharton

GOD'S
PRECIOUS
Promises

Presented to

_____

Compiled by Gary C. Wharton

Cover design by JMK & Associates, Inc.
Book design by Blue Water Ink

Copyright © 1988 by Meridian
Published by Meridian, Grand Rapids, MI
Reprinted 1996 by Meridian, Grand Rapids, MI 49546

M0325
ISBN: 1-56570-032-5

All Scripture is quoted from the King James Version, unless otherwise noted. Contemporary words have been substituted (such as "you" for "ye" and "searches" for "searcheth," etc.) for clarity. Other translations are used by permission.

NASB   New American Standard Bible
NIV   New International Version
RSV   Revised Standard Version

Manufactured in the United States of America

Contents

Promises of Who God Is

Promises of God's Presence with Us

Promises of God's Help

Promises of God's Blessings

Promises to Those Who Follow God's Commands

Promises of the Future

Promises of Who God Is

God Is Faithful

Jehovah Is Promise

Jesus Is Promise

Christ Is Able

God Is Faithful

My God shall supply all your needs according to his riches in glory by Christ Jesus. *Phil. 4:19*

I will not fail you, nor forsake you. *Josh. 1:5*

I will never leave you, nor forsake you. *Heb. 13:5*

Know therefore that the Lord your God, he is God, the faithful God, who keeps covenant and mercy with them that love him and keep his commandments.
Deut. 7:9

He is faithful that promised. *Heb. 10:23*

Faithful is he that calls you, who will also do it. *1 Th. 5:24*

God is faithful, who will not suffer you to be tempted above that which you are able, but with the temptation, provide a way of escape, that you may be able to bear it. *1 Cor. 10:13*

Great is your faithfulness. *Lam. 3:23*

Jehovah Is Promise*

The Lord provides.	*Gen. 22:14*
The Lord heals.	*Ex. 15:26*
The Lord protects.	*Gen. 15:11*
The Lord sanctifies.	*Ex. 31:13*
The Lord sends peace.	*Judg. 6:24*
The Lord of hosts offers strength.	*1 Sam. 1:3*
The Lord is our shepherd.	*Ps. 23:1*
The Lord is our redeemer.	*Isa. 44:24*
The Lord is our righteousness.	*Jer. 23:6*
The Lord is always there.	*Ezek. 48:35*
God the Almighty is all-sufficient.	*Gen. 17:1*
Jehovah is "I am that I am." God is all that we need him to be.	*Ex. 3:14*

* The compounded names of Jehovah God, translated "The Lord," are promises.

Jesus Is Promise

I am the bread of life: he that comes to me shall never hunger: and he that believes on me shall never thirst: . . . if any man eat of this bread, he shall live forever.

Jn. 6:35, 48, 51

I am the light of the world: he that follows me shall not walk in darkness, but shall have the light of life.   *Jn. 8:12*

I am the door. . . by me if any man enter in, he shall be saved. . . . I am come that they might have life, and that they might have it more abundantly.

Jn. 10:7, 9, 10

I am the good shepherd: the good shepherd gives his life for the sheep...

Jn. 10:11

I am the resurrection, and the life: he that believes in me, though he were dead, yet shall he live: and whosoever lives and believes in me shall never die.

Jn. 11:25–26

I am the way, the truth, and the life: no man comes unto the Father, but by me.

Jn. 14:6

I am the true vine, you are the branches: he that abides in me, and I in him, the same brings forth much fruit: for without me you can do nothing. . . . If you abide in me, and my words abide in you, you shall ask what you will, and it shall be done unto you. . . . These things have I spoken unto you, that my joy might remain in you, and that your joy might be full.   *Jn. 15:1–2, 4–5, 7, 9–11*

Christ Is Able

Christ is able to do far more abundantly than all we ask or think. *Eph. 3:20 RSV*

Christ is able for all time to save those who draw near to God through him, since he always lives to make intercession for them. *Heb. 7:25 RSV*

I know whom I have believed, and am persuaded that he is able to keep that which I've committed unto him against that day. *2 Tim. 1:12*

God is able to provide you with every blessing in abundance, so that you may always have enough of everything and may provide in abundance for every good work. *2 Cor. 9:8 RSV*

Now to him who is able to keep you from falling and to present you without blemish for the presence of his glory with rejoicing, to the only God our Savior through Jesus Christ our Lord, be glory, majesty, dominion, and authority, before all time, and now, and for ever. Amen. *Jude 24–25*

Promises *of God's Presence with Us*

Promises of Comfort

He will swallow up death in victory; and the Lord God will wipe away tears off all faces; and the rebuke of his people shall he take away from off all the earth: for the Lord has spoken it. *Isa. 25:8*

As one whom his mother comforts, so will I comfort you. *Isa. 66:13*

Blessed are they that mourn: for they shall be comforted. *Mt. 5:4*

And I will pray the Father, and he shall give you another Comforter, that he may abide with you forever; even the Spirit of truth; whom the world cannot receive, because it sees him not, neither knows him: but you know him; for he dwells with you, and shall be in you. I will not leave you comfortless: I will come to you. *Jn. 14:16–18*

God shall wipe away all tears from their eyes; and there shall be no more death, neither sorrow, nor crying, neither shall there be any more pain: for the former things are passed away. *Rev. 21:4*

Promises of Comfort in Sorrow

Though I walk through the valley of the shadow of death, I will fear no evil: for you are with me; your rod and your staff they comfort me.   *Ps. 23:4*

God is our refuge and our strength, a very present help in trouble.   *Ps. 46:1*

Call upon me in the day of trouble: I will deliver you, and you shall glorify me.
Ps. 50:15

Cast your burden upon the Lord, and he shall sustain you: he shall never suffer the righteous to be moved.   *Ps. 55:22*

The Lord opens the eyes of the blind: the Lord raises them that are bowed down: the Lord loves the righteous. The Lord preserves the strangers; he relieves the fatherless and widows.   *Ps. 146:8–9*

He heals the broken in heart, and binds up their wounds.   *Ps. 147:3*

Fear not: for I have redeemed you, I have called you by your name; you are mine when you pass through the waters, I will be with you: and through the rivers, they shall not overflow you: when you walk through the fire, you shall not be burned; neither shall the flame kindle you.   *Isa. 43:1–2*

Blessed be you poor: for yours is the kingdom of God. Blessed are you that hunger now: for you shall be filled. Blessed are you that weep now: for you shall laugh. Blessed are you, when men shall hate you, and when they shall separate you from their company, and shall reproach you, and cast out your name as evil, for the Son of Man's sake. Rejoice in that day and leap for joy: for behold, your reward is great in Heaven.   *Lu. 6:20–23*

Blessed be God, even the Father of our Lord Jesus Christ, the Father of mercies and the God of all comfort; who comforts us in all our tribulation, that we may be able to comfort them which are in any trouble, by the comfort wherewith we ourselves are comforted of God. For as the sufferings of Christ abound in us, so our consolation abounds by Christ.   *2 Cor. 1:3–5*

Promises of Divine Presence

I am with you and will watch over you wherever you go, and I will bring you back to this land. I will not leave you until I have done what I have promised you.   *Gen. 28:15 NIV*

And the Lord said unto Jacob, Return unto the land of your fathers, and to your kindred: and I will be with you.   *Gen. 31:3*

And He said, My presence shall go with you, and I will give you rest.   *Ex. 33:14*

Be strong and courageous. Do not be afraid or terrified because of them, for the Lord your God goes with you; he will never leave you nor forsake you.
Deut. 31:6 NIV

No one will be able to stand up against you all the days of your life. As I was with Moses, so I will be with you; I will never leave you or forsake you.
Josh. 1:5 NIV

I will dwell among the children of Israel, and will not forsake my people Israel.
1 Kin. 6:13

I am with you says the Lord.   *Hag. 1:13*

For where two or three are gathered together in My name, there I am in the midst of them.   *Mt. 18:20*

Teaching them to observe all things I commanded you: and, lo, I am with you always, even unto the end of the world.   *Mt. 28:20*

Be perfect, be of good comfort, be of one mind, live in peace, and the God of love and peace shall be with you.   *2 Cor. 13:11*

Those things, which you have both learned, and received, and heard, and seen in me, do: and the God of peace shall be with you.   *Phil. 4:9*

Let your conversation be without covetousness; and be content with such things as you have: for He has said, I will never leave you, nor forsake you.   *Heb. 13:5*

Come near to God and He will come near to you.   *Jas. 4:8 NIV*

And I heard a great voice out of heaven saying, Behold, the tabernacle of God is with men, and He will dwell with them, and they shall be his people, and God himself shall be with them, and be their God.   *Rev. 21:3*

Promises to the Faithful

But he that shall endure unto the end, the same shall be saved.   **Mt. 24:13**

Well done, good and faithful servant; you have been faithful over a few things, I will make you ruler over many things; enter into the joy of your Lord.   **Mt. 25:21**

And the Lord said, Who then is that faithful and wise steward, whom his lord shall make ruler over his household, to give them their portion of meat in due season? Blessed is that servant, whom his lord when he comes shall find so doing. Of a truth I say unto you, that he will make him ruler over all that he has.

Lu. 12:42–44

And he said unto him, Well, good servant: because you have been faithful in a very little, you have authority over much.   **Lu. 19:17**

God will render to every man according to his deeds: to them who by patient continuance in well doing seek for glory and honor and immortality, God will render eternal life.   **Rom. 2:6–7**

But glory, honor, and peace, to every man that works good, to the Jew first, and also to the Gentile.   **Rom. 2:10**

Therefore, my beloved brethren, be steadfast, unmovable, always abounding in the work of the Lord, forasmuch as you know that your labor is not in vain in the Lord.

1 Cor. 15:58

And let us not be weary in well doing; for in due season we shall reap, if we faint not.

Gal. 6:9

If we suffer, we shall also reign with him; if we deny him, he will also deny us.

2 Tim. 2:12

Fear none of these things which you shall suffer: behold, the devil shall cast some of you into prison, that you may be tried; and you shall have tribulation ten days: be faithful unto death, and I will give you a crown of life.

Rev. 2:10

Promises of God's Presence

Certainly I will be with you.   *Ex. 3:12*

The Lord, he it is that goes before you; he will be with you, neither forsake you:
fear not, neither be dismayed.   *Deut. 31:8*

God is with you.   *1 Sam. 10:7*

Where two or three are gathered together in my name, there am I in the midst
of them.   *Mt. 18:20*

I am with you always, even unto the end of the world.   *Mt. 28:20*

Peace I leave with you, my peace I give unto you: not as the world gives, give I
unto you. Let not your heart be troubled, neither let it be afraid.   *Jn. 14:27*

Promises of the Holy Spirit

I will pour out my Spirit on all flesh; and your sons and your daughters shall prophesy, your old men shall dream dreams, your young men shall see visions: and also upon the servants and handmaids in those days will I pour out my Spirit. . . . And whosoever shall call upon the name of the Lord shall be delivered.

Joel 2:28–29, 32

If you then, being evil, know how to give good gifts unto your children: how much more shall your heavenly Father give the Holy Spirit to them that ask him?

Lu. 11:13

If any man thirst, let him come unto me, and drink. He that believes on me, as the Scripture has said, out of his belly shall flow rivers of living water. (But this spoke he of the Spirit, which they that believed on him should receive.)

Jn. 7:37–39

And I will pray the Father, and he will give you another Comforter, that he may abide with you forever; even the Spirit of truth; whom the world cannot receive, because it sees him not, neither knows him: but you know him; for he dwells with you, and shall be in you. . . . But the Comforter, which is the Holy Spirit, whom the Father will send in my name, he shall teach you all things to your remembrance, whatsoever I have said unto you. Peace I leave with you, my peace I give unto you: not as the world gives, give I unto you. Let not your heart be troubled, neither let it be afraid. *Jn. 14:16–17, 26–27*

But when the Comforter is come, whom I will send unto you from the Father, even the Spirit of truth, which proceeds from the Father, he shall testify to me. *Jn. 15:26*

It is expedient for you that I go away: for if I go not away, the Comforter will not come unto you; but if I depart, I will send him unto you. *Jn. 16:7*

And you shall receive power, after that the Holy Spirit is come upon you: and you shall be witnesses unto me, both in Jerusalem, and in all Judea, and in Samaria, and unto the uttermost part of the earth. *Ac. 1:8–9*

Repent and be baptized, every one of you in the name of Jesus Christ for the remission of sins, and you shall receive the gift of the Holy Spirit for the promise is unto you, and unto your children, and to all that are afar off, even as many as the Lord our God shall call. *Ac. 2:38–39*

Promises to Those Who Seek God

But if from then you shall seek the Lord your God, you shall find him, if you seek him with all your heart and all your soul.   ***Deut. 4:29***

For the Lord searches all hearts, and understands all the imaginations of the thoughts: if you seek him, he will be found of you.   ***1 Chr. 28:9***

The Lord is with you, while you are with him; and if you seek him, he will be found of you.   ***2 Chr. 15:2***

The hand of our God is upon all them for good that seek him.   ***Ezr. 8:32***

They that seek the Lord shall not lack any good thing.   ***Ps. 34:10***

The Lord is nigh unto all them that call upon him, to all that call upon him in truth.   ***Ps. 145:18***

And you shall seek me, and find me, when you shall search for me with all your heart.   ***Jer. 29:13***

Blessed are they which do hunger and search after righteousness; for they shall be filled.   ***Mt. 5:6***

But seek first the kingdom of God, and his righteousness; and all these things shall be added unto you.   **Mt. 6:33**

Blessed are you that hunger now: for you shall be filled.   **Lu. 6:21**

All that the Father gives me shall come to me; and he that comes to me, I will in no wise cast out.   **Jn. 6:37**

If you shall confess with your mouth, the Lord Jesus, and shall believe in your heart that God has raised him from the dead, you shall be saved. For with the heart men believe unto righteousness; and with the mouth confession is made unto salvation . . . for whosoever shall call upon the name of the Lord shall be saved.   **Rom. 10:9–10, 13**

Now faith is the substance of things hoped for, the evidence of things not seen. . . . Through faith we understand that the world was framed by the word of God. . . . But without faith it is impossible to please him: for he that comes to God must believe that he is, and that he is a rewarder of them that diligently seek him.   **Heb. 11:1, 3, 6**

Promises of Spiritual Enlightenment

In that day shall the deaf hear the words of the book, and the eyes of the blind shall see out of obscurity, and out of darkness. . . . They also that erred in spirit shall come to understanding, and they that murmured shall learn doctrine.

Isa. 92:18, 24

Be strong, fear not: behold, your God will come with vengeance, even God with a recompense; he will come and save you. Then the eyes of the blind shall be opened, and the ears of the deaf shall be unstopped. Then shall the lame man leap as a hart, and the tongue of the dumb sing; for in the wilderness shall waters break forth as streams in the desert.

Isa. 35:4–6

And I will bring the blind by a way that they know not; I will lead them in paths that they have not known: I will make a darkness light before them, and crooked things straight. These things I will do unto them, and not forsake them. . . . Hear, you deaf; and look, you blind, that you may see!

Isa. 42:16, 18

But when they deliver you up, be not anxious how or what you shall speak: for it shall be given you in that same hour what you shall speak.

Mt. 10:19

Settle it therefore in your hearts, not to meditate before what you shall answer:

for I will give you a mouth of wisdom, which all your adversaries shall not be able to gainsay or resist. *Lu. 21:14–15*

My teaching is not mine, but him that sent me. If any man wills to do his will, he shall know of the teaching, whether it be of God, or whether I speak of myself. *Jn. 7:16–17*

I am the light of the world: he that follows me shall not walk in the darkness, but shall have the light of life. . . . And you shall know the truth, and the truth shall make you free. *Jn. 8:12, 32*

I have come into the world as a light, so that no one who believes in me should stay in darkness. *Jn. 12:46 NIV*

Promises of God's Help

Promises of Answer to Prayer

Promises to the Burdened and Afflicted

Promises of Divine Guidance

Promises of Divine Help

Promises to Orphans and Widows

Promises to Persecuted Believers

Promises to the Poor

Promises of Providential Care

Promises of Refuge in Adversity

Promises of Security

Promises of Deliverance from Trouble

Promises of Deliverance from Temptation

Promises of Answer to Prayer

If my people, which are called by my name, shall humble themselves, and pray, and seek my face, and turn from their wicked ways; then will I hear from heaven, and will forgive their sin, and will heal their land.   *2 Chr. 7:14*

You shall make your prayer unto him, and he shall hear you.   *Job 22:27*

Ask of me, and I will make the nations your heritage, and the ends of the earth your possession.   *Ps. 2:8 RSV*

He will fulfill the desire of them that fear him: he will also hear their cry, and will save them.   *Ps. 145:19*

The Lord is far from the wicked: but he hears the prayer of the righteous. *Pr. 15:29*

Then shall you call, and the Lord will answer; you shall cry, and he shall say, Here I am.   *Isa. 58:9*

Before they call, I will answer; and while they are yet speaking, I will hear.   *Isa. 65:24*

Then shall you call upon me, and you shall go and pray unto me, and I will hearken unto you. *Jer. 29:12*

Call unto me, and I will answer you, and show you great and mighty things, which you know not. *Jer. 33:3*

When you pray, enter into your closet, and when you have shut the door, pray to the Father which is in secret; and your Father which sees in secret shall reward you openly. *Mt. 6:6*

Ask, and it shall be given you; seek, and you shall find; knock, and it shall be opened unto you. For every one that asks, receives; and he that seeks, finds; and to him that knocks, it shall be opened . . . . How much more shall your Father which is in heaven give good things to them that ask him? *Mt. 7:7–8, 11*

All things whatsoever you shall ask in prayer, believing, you shall receive. *Mt. 11:24*

If two of you shall agree on earth as touching anything that they shall ask, it shall be done for them of my Father which is in heaven. For where two or three are gathered together in my name, there am I in the midst. *Mt. 18:19–20*

With God all things are possible. *Mt. 19:26*

And all things, whatsoever you shall ask in prayer, believing, you shall receive.

Mt. 21:22

Truly I say to you, whoever says to this mountain, be taken up and cast into the sea, and does not doubt in his heart, but believes that what he says will come to pass, it will be done for him. Therefore I tell you, whatever you ask in prayer, believe that you have received it, and it will be yours.

Mk. 11:23–24 RSV

And whatsoever you shall ask in my name, that will I do, that the Father may be glorified in the Son: if you ask anything in my name, I will do it.

Jn. 14:13–14

If you abide in me, and my words abide in you, ask what you will, and it shall be done unto you.

Jn. 15:7

You have not chosen me, but I have chosen you, and ordained you, that you should go and bring forth fruit, and that your fruit should remain: that whatsoever you shall ask of the Father in my name, he may give it to you.

Jn. 15:16

My Father will give you whatever you ask in my name. Until now you have not asked for anything in my name. Ask and you will receive, and your joy will be complete.

Jn. 16:23–24 NIV

Your prayers and gifts to the poor have come up as a remembrance before God.

Ac. 10:4 NIV

If any of you lack wisdom, let him ask of God, that gives to all men liberally, and upbraids not: and it shall be given him.

Jas. 1:5

The prayer of faith shall save the sick, and the Lord shall raise him up; and if he has committed sins, they shall be forgiven him. The effectual fervent prayer of a righteous man avails much.

Jas. 5:15–16

And whatsoever we ask, we receive of him, because we keep his commandments, and do those things that are pleasing in his sight.

1 Jn. 3:22

And this is the confidence that we have in him, that, if we ask anything according to his will, he hears us.

1 Jn. 5:14

Promises to the Burdened and Afflicted

He will deliver his soul from going into the pit, and his life shall see the light.

Job 33:28

He delivers the poor in his affliction, and opens their ears in oppression. *Job 36:15*

The Lord also will be a refuge for the oppressed, and refuge in time of trouble.

Ps. 9:9

For the oppression of the poor, for the sighing of the needy, now will I arise, says the Lord; I will set him in safety from him that threatens him. *Ps. 12:5*

For you will save the afflicted people; for they will light my candle: the Lord my God will enlighten my darkness. *Ps. 18:27–28*

The Lord sustains him on his sickbed; in his illness the Lord heals all his infirmities. *Ps. 41:3 RSV*

Come unto me, all you that labor and are heavy laden, and I will give you rest. Take my yoke upon you, and learn of me; for I am meek and lowly of heart: and you shall find rest unto your souls. For my yoke is easy, and my burden is light.

Mt. 11:28–30

Promises of Divine Guidance

What man is he that fears the Lord? Him shall he teach in the way that he shall choose.
Ps. 25:12

The steps of a good man are ordered by the Lord: and he delights in his way. Though he fall, he shall not be utterly cast down: for the Lord upholds him with his hand.
Ps. 37:23–24

For this God is our God for ever and ever: he will be our guide even unto death.
Ps. 48:14

You shall guide me with your counsel, and afterward receive me to glory.
Ps. 73:24

Trust in the Lord with all your heart; and lean not unto your own understanding. In all your ways acknowledge him, and he shall direct your paths.
Pr. 3:5–6

Promises of Divine Help

The Lord will give strength unto his people; the Lord will bless his people with peace.   *Ps. 29:11*

Cast your burden upon the Lord, and he shall sustain you: he shall never suffer the righteous to be moved.   *Ps. 55:22*

So do not fear, for I am with you; do not be dismayed, for I am your God. I will strengthen you and help you; I will uphold you with my righteous right hand. All who rage against you will surely be ashamed and disgraced; those who oppose you will be as nothing and perish. . . . For I am the Lord, your God, who takes hold of your right hand and says to you, Do not fear; I will help you. *Isa. 41:10–11, 13 NIV*

And he said unto me, My grace is sufficient for you: for my strength is made perfect in weakness. Most gladly therefore will I rather glory in my infirmities, that the power of Christ may rest upon me.   *2 Cor. 12:9*

But my God shall supply all your needs according to his riches in glory by Christ Jesus.   *Phil. 4:19*

The Lord is my helper, and I will not fear what man shall do unto me. *Heb. 13:6*

Promises to Orphans and Widows

He executes justice for the fatherless and widowed, and loves the stranger.

Deut. 10:18

A father of the fatherless, and a protector of the widows, is God in his holy habitation.

Ps. 68:5

The Lord preserves the strangers; he upholds the fatherless and the widow.

Ps. 146:9

The Lord will destroy the house of the proud: but he will establish the border of the widow.

Pr. 15:25

Promises to Persecuted Believers

Blessed are they which are persecuted for righteousness' sake: for theirs is the kingdom of heaven. Blessed are you, when men shall revile you, and persecute you, and shall say all manner of evil against you falsely, for my sake.

Mt. 5:10–11

And you shall be hated of all men for my name's sake: but he that endures to the end shall be saved.
Mt. 10:22

Blessed are you, when men shall hate you, and when they shall separate you from their company, and shall reproach you, and cast out your name as evil, for the Son of Man's sake. Rejoice in that day, and leap for joy: for, behold, your reward is great in heaven: for in the like manner did their fathers unto the prophets.
Lu. 6:22–23

For I will give you a mouth and wisdom, which all your adversaries shall not be able to rebuke nor resist. And you shall be betrayed both by parents, and brethren, and kinfolks, and friends: and some of you shall they cause to be put to death. And you shall be hated of all men for my name's sake. But there shall not a hair of your head perish.
Lu. 21:15–18

For our light affliction, which is but for a moment, works for us a far more exceeding and eternal weight of glory. *2 Cor. 4:17*

If you suffer for righteousness' sake, happy are you: and be not afraid of their terror, neither be troubled. *1 Pet. 3:14*

If you are reproached for the name of Christ, happy are you; for the spirit of glory and of God rests upon you: on their part he is evil spoken of, but on your part he is glorified. *1 Pet. 4:14*

Fear none of those things which you shall suffer: behold, the devil shall cast some of you into prison, that you may be tried; and you shall have tribulation ten days: be faithful unto death, and I will give you a crown of life. *Rev. 2:10*

Promises to the Poor

It shall come to pass, when he cries unto me, that I will hear; for I am gracious.

Ex. 22:27

He delivers the poor in his affliction, and opens their ears in oppression. *Job 36:15*

For the oppression of the poor, for the sighing of the needy, now will I arise, says the Lord; I will set him in safety from him that threatens him.

Ps. 12:5

All my bones shall say, Lord, who is like unto you, which delivers the poor from him that is too strong for him, yea, the poor and the needy from him that spoils him?

Ps. 35:10

For the Lord hears the poor, and despises not his prisoners.

Ps. 69:33

He shall judge the people with righteousness, and the poor with judgment. . . . He shall judge the poor of the people, he shall save the children of the needy, and shall break in pieces the oppressor.

Ps. 72:2, 4

For he shall deliver the needy when he cries; the poor also, and him that has no helper. He shall spare the poor and needy, and shall save the souls of the needy.

Ps. 72:12–13

For he shall stand at the right hand of the poor, to save him from those that condemn his soul.   *Ps. 109:31*

I will abundantly bless her provision: I will satisfy her poor with bread.
Ps. 132:15

Rob not the poor, because he is poor: neither oppress the afflicted in the gate: for the Lord will plead their cause, and spoil the soul of those that spoiled them.
Pr. 22:22–23

When the poor and needy seek water, and there is none, and their tongue fails for thirst, I the Lord will hear them, I the God of Israel will not forsake them.
Isa. 41:17

Promises of Providential Care

After these things the word of the Lord came unto Abraham in a vision, saying, Fear not, Abraham: I am your shield, and your exceeding great reward.

Gen. 15:1

But if you shall indeed obey his voice, and do all that I speak; then I will be an enemy unto your enemies, and an adversary unto your adversaries.   *Ex. 23:22*

Your threshing will continue until grape harvest and the grape harvest will continue until planting, and you will eat all the food you want and live in safety in your land. I will grant peace in the land, and you will lie down and no one will make you afraid. I will remove savage beasts from the land, and the sword will not pass through your country. You will still be eating last year's harvest when you will have to move it out to make room for the new.   *Lev. 26:5, 6, 10 NIV*

The eternal God is your refuge, and underneath are the everlasting arms: and he shall thrust out the enemy from before you; and shall say, Destroy them!

Deut. 33:27

He will keep the feet of his saints, and the wicked shall be silent in darkness; for by strength shall no man prevail.   *1 Sam. 2:9*

The hand of our God is upon all them for good that seek him; but his power and his wrath is against all them that forsake him.   *Ezr. 8:22*

O fear the Lord, you his saints, for there is no want to them that fear him. The young lions do lack, and suffer hunger: but they that seek the Lord shall not lack any good thing.   *Ps. 34:9–10*

The steps of a good man are ordered by the Lord: and he delights in his way. Though he fall, he shall not be utterly cast down: for the Lord upholds him with his hand. I have been young, and now am old; yet have I not seen the righteous forsaken, nor his seed begging bread. He is ever merciful and lends; and his seed is blessed.   *Ps. 37:23–26*

The Lord shall preserve you from all evil: He shall preserve your soul. The Lord shall preserve your going out and your coming in from this time forth, and even for evermore.   *Ps. 121:7–8*

They that trust in the Lord shall be as Mount Zion, which cannot be removed, but abides forever. As the mountains are round about Jerusalem, so the Lord is round about his people from henceforth ever for ever.   *Ps. 125:1–3*

He will fulfill the desire of them that fear him: he also will hear their cry, and will save them. The Lord preserves all them that love him: but all the wicked will he destroy. *Ps. 145:19–20*

Whoever listens to me will live in safety and be at ease, without fear of harm. *Pr. 1:33 NIV*

He holds victory in store for the upright, he is a shield to those whose walk is blameless. *Pr. 2:7 NIV*

In all your ways acknowledge him, and he shall direct your paths. *Pr. 3:6*

The Lord will not suffer the soul of the righteous to famish: but he casts away the substance of the wicked. *Pr. 10:3*

When a man's ways please the Lord, he makes even his enemies to be at peace with him. *Pr. 16:7*

But even the very hairs of your head are all numbered. Fear not therefore, you are of more value than many sparrows. *Lu. 12:7*

Cast all your cares upon him, for he cares for you. *1 Pet. 5:7*

Promises of Refuge in Adversity

Behold, the eye of the Lord is upon them that fear him, upon them that hope in his mercy; to deliver their soul from death, and to keep them alive in famine.

Ps. 33:18–19

Trust in the Lord at all times: pour out your heart before him: God is a refuge for us.

Ps. 62:8

He that dwells in the secret place of the Most High shall abide under the shadow of the Almighty.

Ps. 91:1

Surely he will save you from the fowler's snare and from the deadly pestilence. He will cover you with his feathers, and under his wings you will find refuge; his faithfulness will be your shield and rampart. You will not fear the terror of night, nor the arrow that flies by day, nor the pestilence that stalks in the darkness, nor the plague that destroys at midday. A thousand may fall at your side, ten thousand at your right hand, but it will not come near you.

Ps. 91:3–7 NIV

If you make the Most High your dwelling—even the Lord, who is my refuge—then no harm will befall you, no disaster will come near your tent. For he will command his angels concerning you to guard you in all your ways; they will lift you up in their hands, so that you will not strike your foot against a stone.

Ps. 91:9–12 NIV

In the fear of the Lord is strong confidence: and his children shall have a place of refuge.

Pr. 14:26

Promises of Security

For this shall every one that is godly pray unto you in a time when you may be found: surely in the floods of great waters they shall not come nigh unto him. You are my hiding place; you shall preserve me from trouble: you shall compass me about with songs of deliverance.   **Ps. 32:6–7**

For the Lord God is a sun and shield: the Lord will give grace and glory: no good thing will he withhold from them that walk uprightly.   **Ps. 84:11**

The Lord shall preserve you from all evil: He shall preserve your soul. The Lord shall preserve your going out and your coming in from this time forth, and even for evermore.   **Ps. 121:7–8**

This is the man who will dwell on the heights, whose refuge will be the mountain fortress. His bread will be supplied, and water will not fail him.   **Isa. 33:16 NIV**

Promises of Deliverance from Trouble

Behold, the eye of the Lord is upon them that fear him, upon them that hope in his mercy; to deliver their soul from death, and to keep them alive in famine.

Ps. 33:18–19

The eyes of the Lord are upon the righteous, and his ears are open unto their cry. The righteous cry, and the Lord hears, and delivers them out of all their troubles.

Ps. 34:15, 17

Call upon me in the day of trouble: I will deliver you, and you shall glorify me.

Ps. 50:15

You that love the Lord, hate evil: he preserves the souls of his saints; he delivers them out of the hand of the wicked.

Ps. 97:10

Be not afraid of sudden fear, neither of the desolation of the wicked, when it comes. For the Lord shall be your confidence, and shall keep your foot from being taken.

Pr. 3:25–26

So do not fear, for I am with you; do not be dismayed, for I am your God. I will strengthen you and help you; I will uphold you with my righteous right hand.

All who rage against you will surely be ashamed and disgraced; those who oppose you will be as nothing and perish. Though you search for your enemies, you will not find them. Those who wage war against you will be as nothing at all. For I am the Lord, your God, who takes hold of your right hand and says to you, Do not fear; I will help you.   *Isa. 41:10–13 NIV*

When you pass through the waters, I will be with you; and through the rivers, they shall not overflow you: when you walk through the fire, you shall not be burned; neither shall the flame kindle upon you.   *Isa. 43:2*

Promises of Deliverance From Temptation

There has no temptation taken you but such as is common to man: but God is faithful, who will not allow you to be tempted above that you are able; but will with the temptation also make a way to escape, that you may be able to bear it.

1 Cor. 10:13

Submit yourselves therefore to God. Resist the devil, and he will flee from you.

Jas. 4:7

The Lord knows how to deliver the godly out of temptation, and to reserve the unjust unto the day of judgment to be punished.

2 Pet. 2:9

Promises of God's Blessings

Promises to Backsliders

Promises of Blessings on Our Children

Promises to Children

Promises to Those Who Endure

Promises of God's Forgiveness

Promises of God's Goodness

Promises of Peace

Promises of Prosperity

Promises of Salvation

Promises of Spiritual Adoption

Promises of Wisdom

Promises to Backsliders

When you shall return unto the Lord your God, and shall obey his voice with all your heart, and with all your soul; then the Lord your God will have compassion upon you, and will return and gather you from all the nations, wherever the Lord your God has scattered you.   *Deut. 30:2–3*

If my people, which are called by my name, shall humble themselves, and pray, and seek my face, and turn from their wicked ways; then will I hear from heaven, and will forgive their sin, and I will heal their land.   *2 Chr. 7:14*

The Lord your God is gracious and merciful, and will not turn away his face from you, if you return unto him.   *2 Chr. 30:9*

Return, you backsliding Israel, says the Lord; and I will not cause my anger to fall upon you: for I am merciful, says the Lord, and I will not keep anger forever. Only acknowledge your iniquity, that you have transgressed against the Lord your God, and have scattered your ways to the strangers under every green tree, and you have not obeyed my voice, says the Lord. Turn, O backsliding children, says the Lord; for I am married unto you: and I will take you one of a city, and two of a family, and I will bring you to Zion: and I will give you shepherds according to my heart, which shall feed you with knowledge and understanding.

Jer. 3:12–15

I will heal their backsliding, I will love them freely: for my anger is turned away from him.

Hos. 14:4

Return unto me, and I will return unto you, says the Lord of hosts.

Mal. 3:7

Promises of Blessings on Our Children

But the mercy of the Lord is from everlasting to everlasting upon them that fear him, and his righteousness unto children's children.   **Ps. 103:17**

His children will be mighty in the land; each generation of the upright will be blessed. Wealth and riches are in his house, and his righteousness endures forever.   **Ps. 112:2–3 NIV**

As for me, this is my covenant with them, says the Lord. My spirit, who is on you, and my words that I have put in your mouth will not depart from your mouth, or from the mouths of your children, or from the mouths of their descendants from this time on and forever, says the Lord.   **Isa. 59:21 NIV**

Promises to Children

Honor your father and your mother: that your days may be long upon the land which the Lord your God gives you.
Ex. 20:12

Honor your father and your mother, as the Lord your God has commanded you; that your days may be prolonged, and that it may go well with you, in the land which the Lord your God gives you.
Deut. 5:16

Jesus said: Let the children come to me, and do not hinder them; for to such belongs the kingdom of heaven.
Mt. 19:14; Mk. 10:14

Whosoever shall not receive the kingdom of God as a little child shall in no wise enter therein.
Lu. 18:17

Children, obey your parents in the Lord: for this is right. Honor your father and mother; which is the first commandment with promise; that it may be well with you, and you may live long on the earth.
Eph. 6:1–3

Promises to Those Who Endure

And you shall be hated of all men for my name's sake: but he that endures to the end shall be saved.
Mt. 10:22

But he that shall endure unto the end, the same shall be saved.
Mt. 24:13

To him that overcomes will I give to eat of the tree of life, which is in the midst of the paradise of God.
Rev. 2:7

And he that overcomes, and keeps my works unto the end, to him will I give power over the nations.
Rev. 2:26

He that overcomes, the same shall be clothed in white raiment; and I will not blot out his name out of the book of life, but I will confess his name before my Father, and before his angels.
Rev. 3:5

He that overcomes will I make a pillar in the temple of my God, and he shall go no more out: and I will write upon him the name of my God, and the name of the city of my God, which is new Jerusalem, which comes down out of heaven from my God: and I will write upon him my new name.
Rev. 3:12

To him that overcomes will I grant to sit with me in my throne, even as I also overcame, and am set down with my Father in his throne. *Rev. 3:21*

He that overcomes shall inherit all things; and I will be his God, and he shall be my son. *Rev. 21:7*

Promises of God's Forgiveness

Come, let us reason together, says the Lord: though your sins be as scarlet, they shall be white as snow; though they be red as crimson, they shall be as wool.

Isa. 1:18

I, even I, am he that blots out your transgressions for mine own sake, and will not remember your sins.

Isa. 43:25

Seek the Lord while he may be found. Call upon him while he is near: let the wicked forsake his way, and the unrighteous man his thoughts: and let him return unto the Lord, and he will have mercy upon him: and to our God, and will abundantly pardon.

Isa. 55:6–7

I will forgive their iniquity, and I will remember their sins no more.

Jer. 31:34

And I will cleanse them from all iniquity, whereby they have sinned against me; and I will pardon all their iniquities, whereby they have sinned, and whereby they have transgressed against me.

Jer. 33:8

For if you forgive men their trespasses, your heavenly Father will also forgive you.

Mt. 6:14

Through Jesus' name, whosoever believes in him shall receive remission of sins.

Ac. 10:43

Through Jesus is preached unto you forgiveness of sins. *Ac. 13:38*

The prayer of faith shall save the sick, and the Lord shall raise him up; and if he has committed sins, they shall be forgiven him. Confess your faults one to another, and pray for one another, that you may be healed. *Jas. 5:15–16*

If we confess our sins, he is faithful and just to forgive us our sins, and to cleanse us from all unrighteousness. *1 Jn. 1:9*

Promises of God's Goodness

For since the beginning of the world men have not heard, nor perceived by the ear, neither has the eye seen, O God, besides you, what he has prepared for him that waits for him.   *Isa. 64:4*

And we know that all things work together for good to them that love God, to them who are the called according to his purpose.   *Rom. 8:28*

Eye has not seen, nor ear heard, neither have entered into the heart of man, the things which God has prepared for them that love him.   *1 Cor. 2:9*

For our light affliction, which is but for a moment, works for us a far more exceeding and eternal weight of glory.   *2 Cor. 4:17*

Promises of Peace

You will keep him in perfect peace, whose mind is stayed on you: because he trusts in you.

Isa. 26:3

Peace I leave with you, my peace I give unto you: not as the world gives, give I unto you. Let not your heart be troubled, neither let it be afraid.

Jn. 14:27

These things I have spoken unto you, that in me you might have peace. In the world you shall have tribulation: but be of good cheer; I have overcome the world.

Jn. 16:33

Glory, honor, and peace, for everyone who does good: first for the Jew, then for the Gentile.

Rom. 2:10 NIV

Therefore, being justified by faith, we have peace with God through our Lord Jesus Christ.

Rom. 5:1

For he himself is our peace, who has made the two one and has destroyed the barrier, the dividing wall of hostility.

Eph. 2:14 NIV

Promises of Prosperity

Wherefore you shall do my statutes, and keep my judgments, and do them; and you shall dwell in the land in safety. And the land shall yield her fruit, and you shall eat your fill, and dwell therein in safety.   *Lev. 25:18–19*

Your threshing will continue until grape harvest and the grape harvest will continue until planting and you will eat all the food you want and live in safety in your land.   *Lev. 26:5 NIV*

For evildoers shall be cut off: but those that wait upon the Lord, they shall inherit the earth.   *Ps. 37:9*

Blessed is everyone that fears the Lord; that walks in his ways. For you shall eat the labor of your hands: happy shall you be, and it shall be well with you.
          Ps. 128:1–2

For the upright shall dwell in the land, and the perfect shall remain in it.
          Pr. 2:21

My son, do not forget my teaching, but keep my commands in your heart, for they will prolong your life many years and bring you prosperity. Let love and faithfulness never leave you; bind them around your neck, write them on the tablet of your heart. Then you will win favor and a good name in the sight of God and man. *Pr. 3:1–4 NIV*

Do not be wise in your own eyes; fear the Lord and shun evil. This will bring health to your body and nourishment to your bones. Honor the Lord with your wealth, with the firstfruits of all your crops; then your barns will be filled to overflowing, and your vats will brim over with new wine. *Pr. 3:7–10 NIV*

Seek first his kingdom and his righteousness, and all these things will be added unto you. *Mt. 6:33*

Verily I say unto you, there is no man that has left his house, or parents, or brethren, or wife, or children, for the kingdom of God's sake, who shall not receive manifold more in this present time, and in the world to come life everlasting. *Lu. 18:29–30*

Promises of Salvation

Look unto me, and be saved, all the ends of the earth: for I am God, and there is none else.
Isa. 45:22

For God so loved the world, that he gave his only begotten Son, that whosoever believes in him should not perish, but have everlasting life. For God sent not his Son into the world to condemn the world; but that the world through him might be saved.
Jn. 3:16–17

And it shall come to pass, that whosoever shall call on the name of the Lord shall be saved.
Ac. 2:21

Believe on the Lord Jesus Christ and you shall be saved.
Act. 16:31

For whosoever shall call upon the name of the Lord shall be saved.
Rom. 10:13

For by grace are you saved through faith; and that not of yourselves: it is the gift of God.
Eph. 2:8

Promises of Spiritual Adoption

I will walk among you, and will be your God, and you shall be my people.

Lev. 26:12

But as many as received him, to them gave he power to become the sons of God, even to them that believe on his name; which were born, not of blood, nor of the will of the flesh, nor of the will of man, but of God. *Jn. 1:12–13*

For as many as are led by the Spirit of God, they are the sons of God. . . . You have received the Spirit of adoption, whereby we cry, Abba, Father. The Spirit himself bears witness with our spirit, that we are the children of God: and if children, then heirs; heirs of God, and joint-heirs with Christ; and if so be that we suffer with him, that we may be also glorified together. *Rom. 8:14–17*

Wherefore come out from among them, and be separate, says the Lord; . . . and I will receive you, and will be a Father unto you, and you shall be my sons and daughters, says the Lord Almighty. *2 Cor. 6:17–18*

For you are all the children of God by faith in Christ Jesus. . . . And if you be Christ's, then you are heirs according to the promise. *Gal. 3:26, 29*

When the fullness of time was come, God sent forth his Son, born of a woman, born under the law, to redeem them that were under the law, that we might receive the adoption of sons. Wherefore as you are no more a servant, but a son; and if a son, then an heir of God, through Christ Jesus. *Gal. 4:4–5, 7*

Blessed be the God and Father of our Lord Jesus Christ, who has blessed us with all spiritual blessings in heavenly places in Christ: accordingly as he has chosen us in him before the foundation of the world, that we should be holy and without blemish before him in love: having predestined us unto the adoption of children by Jesus Christ to himself, . . . wherein he has made us accepted in the beloved. In whom we have redemption through his blood, the forgiveness of sins, according to the riches of his grace. *Eph. 1:3–7*

Promises of Wisdom

For the Lord gives wisdom: out of his mouth comes knowledge and understanding.

Pr. 2:6

When wisdom enters into your heart, and knowledge is pleasant unto your soul; discretion shall preserve you, understanding shall keep you.

Pr. 2:10–11

If any of you lack wisdom, let him ask of God, that gives to all men liberally, and upbraids not; and it shall be given him.

Jas. 1:5

Promises *to Those Who Follow God's Commands*

Promises to Believers

Promises to Those Who Confess Christ

Promises to the Forgiving

Promises to the Humble

Promises to the Liberal Giver

Promises to Those Who Love Their Enemies

Promises to the Meek

Promises to the Merciful

Promises to the Ministers

Promises to the Obedient

Promises to the Repentant

Promises to Those Who Reverence God

Promises to the Righteous

Promises to Believers

Blessed is the man that trusts in the Lord and whose hope the Lord is. For he shall be as a tree planted by the waters, and spreads out her roots by the river, and shall not fear when heat comes, but her leaf shall be green; and shall not be full of care in the year of drought, neither shall cease from yielding fruit.

Jer. 17:7–8

But as many as received him, to them gave he power to become the sons of God, even to them that believe on his name.

Jn. 1:12

Whosoever believes in him should not perish, but have eternal life. For God so loved the world, that he gave his only begotten Son, that whosoever believes on him should not perish, but have everlasting life.

Jn. 3:15–16

He that hears my word, and believes on him that sent me, has everlasting life, and he will not come into condemnation, but is passed from death into life.

Jn. 5:24

I am the bread of life: he that comes to me shall never hunger; and he that believes on me shall never thirst. . . . Everyone which sees the Son, and believes on him, may have everlasting life: and I will raise him up in the last day. . . . He that believes on me has everlasting life. *Jn. 6:35, 40, 47*

I am the resurrection, and the life: he that believes in me, though he were dead, yet shall he live. And whosoever lives and believes on me shall never die. *Jn. 11:25–26*

He that believes on me, the works that I do shall he do also; and greater works than these shall he do; because I go unto my Father. And whatsoever you shall ask in my name, that will I do, that the Father may be glorified in the Son. If you shall ask any thing in my name, I will do it. *Jn. 14:12–14*

Whosoever believes on him shall not be ashamed. *Rom 9:33*

If you shall confess with your mouth the Lord Jesus, and shall believe in your heart that God has raised him from the dead, you shall be saved. For with the heart man believes unto righteousness; and with the mouth confession is made unto salvation. For the scripture says, whosoever believes on him shall not be ashamed. . . . For whosoever shall call upon the name of the Lord shall be saved. *Rom. 10:9–13*

Promises to Those Who Confess Christ

Whosoever therefore shall confess me before men, him will I confess also before my Father which is in heaven.   *Mt. 10:32*

That if you shall confess with your mouth the Lord Jesus and shall believe in your heart that God has raised him from the dead, you shall be saved. *Rom. 10:9*

Whosoever denies the Son, the same has not the Father: but he that acknowledges the Son has the Father also.   *1 Jn. 2:23*

Whosoever shall confess that Jesus is the Son of God, God dwells in him, and he in God.   *1 Jn. 4:15*

Promises to the Forgiving

For if you forgive men for their trespasses, your heavenly Father will also forgive you. *Mt. 6:14*

And when you stand praying, forgive, if you have anything against any; that your Father also which is in Heaven may forgive you your trespasses. *Mk. 11:25*

Judge not, and you shall not be judged; condemn not, and you shall not be condemned; forgive, and you shall be forgiven. *Lu. 6:37*

And be kind one to another, tenderhearted, forgiving one another, even as God for Christ's sake has forgiven you. *Eph. 4:32*

Forbearing one another, and forgiving one another, if any man have a quarrel against any, even as Christ forgave you, you also do. *Col. 3:13*

Promises to the Humble

When men are cast down, then you shall say, there is lifting up; and he shall save the humble person.
Job 22:29

Though the Lord be high, yet has he respect unto the lowly; but the proud he knows afar off.
Ps. 138:6

The fear of the Lord is in the instruction of wisdom; and before honor is humility.
Pr. 15:33

A man's pride shall bring him low; but honor shall uphold the humble in spirit.
Pr. 29:23

For thus says the high and lofty One that inhabits eternity, whose name is Holy: I dwell in the high and holy place, with him also that is of a contrite and humble spirit, to revive the spirit of the humble, and to revive the heart of the contrite ones.
Isa. 57:15

Blessed are the humble in spirit; for theirs is the kingdom of heaven.
Mt. 5:3

Whosoever therefore shall humble himself as this little child, the same is greatest in the kingdom of heaven.
Mt. 18:4

And whosoever shall exalt himself shall be abased; and he that shall humble himself shall be exalted.   *Mt. 23:12*

God resists the proud, but gives grace unto the humble.   *Jas. 4:6*

Promises to the Liberal Giver

Blessed is he that considers the poor: the Lord will deliver him in time of trouble. The Lord will preserve him and keep him alive; and he shall be blessed upon the earth; and you will not deliver him unto the will of his enemies. *Ps. 41:1–2*

He has dispersed, he has given to the poor; his righteousness endures for ever; his horn shall be exalted with honor. *Ps. 112:9*

Honor the Lord with your substance, and with the firstfruits of all your increase. So shall your barns be filled with plenty, and your presses shall burst out with new wine. *Pr. 3:9–10*

The liberal soul shall be made fat; and he that waters shall be watered also himself. *Pr. 11:25*

He that has a bountiful eye shall be blessed; for he gives of his bread to the poor. *Pr. 22:9*

He that gives unto the poor shall not lack; but he that hides his eyes shall have many a curse. *Pr. 28:27*

Cast your bread upon the waters; for you shall find it after many days. *Ec. 11:1*

And if you draw out your soul to the hungry, and satisfy the afflicted soul; then shall your light rise in obscurity, and your darkness be as the noonday. And the Lord shall guide you continually, and satisfy your soul in drought, and make fat your bones; and you shall be like a garden, and like a spring of water, whose waters fail not.

Isa. 58:10–11

That your alms may be in secret; and your Father which sees in secret himself shall reward you openly.

Mt. 6:4

Give, and it shall be given unto you.

Lu. 6:38

But this I say, he which sows sparingly shall also reap sparingly; and he which sows bountifully shall also reap bountifully.

2 Cor. 9:6

And God is able to make all grace abound toward you; that you, always having all sufficiency in all things, may abound to every good work.

2 Cor. 9:8

Promises to Those Who Love Their Enemies

Blessed are the peacemakers: for they shall be called the children of God.

Mt. 5:9

But I say unto you, Love your enemies, bless them that curse you, do good to them that hate you, and pray for them which despitefully use you, and persecute you; that you may be the children of your Father which is in heaven: for he makes his sun to rise on the evil and on the good, and sends rain on the just and on the unjust.

Mt. 5:44–45

But I say unto you which hear, Love your enemies, and do good to them which hate you.

Lu. 6:27

Bless them which persecute you: bless, and curse not.

Rom. 12:14

Promises to the Meek

Lord, you have heard the desire of the humble; you will prepare their heart, you will cause your ear to hear. **Ps. 10:17**

The meek shall eat and be satisfied: they shall praise the Lord that seek him: your heart shall live for ever. **Ps. 22:26**

But the meek shall inherit the earth; and shall delight themselves in the abundance of peace. **Ps. 37:11**

The Lord lifts up the meek; he casts the wicked down to the ground. **Ps. 147:6**

For the Lord takes pleasure in his people; he will beautify the meek with salvation. **Ps. 149:4**

A man's pride shall bring him low, but honor shall uphold the humble in spirit. **Pr. 29:23**

The meek also shall increase their joy in the Lord, and the poor among men shall rejoice in the Holy One of Israel. **Isa. 29:19**

Blessed are the meek, for they shall inherit the earth. **Mt. 5:5**

Promises to the Merciful

With the merciful you will show yourself merciful, and with the upright man you will show yourself upright.   **2 Sam. 22:26**

Blessed is he that considers the poor: the Lord will deliver him in time of trouble. The Lord will preserve him and keep him alive; and he shall be blessed upon the earth: and you will not deliver him unto the will of his enemies.   **Ps. 41:1–2**

Blessed are the merciful: for they shall obtain mercy.   **Mt. 5:7**

Promises to Ministers

They that sow in tears shall reap in joy. He that goes forth weeping, bearing precious seed, shall doubtless come again with rejoicing, bringing his sheaves with him.   *Ps. 126:5–6*

Be not afraid of their faces: for I am with you to deliver you, says the Lord.
                                                                                Jer. 1:8

But the Lord is with me as a mighty terrible one: therefore my prosecutors shall stumble, and they shall not prevail: they shall be greatly ashamed; for they shall not prosper: their everlasting confusion shall never be forgotten.   *Jer. 20:11*

And they that be wise shall shine as the brightness of the firmament; and they that turn many to righteousness as the stars for ever and ever.   *Dan. 12:3*

Teaching them to observe all things whatsoever I have commanded you: and, lo, I am with you alway, even unto the end of the world.   *Mt. 28:20*

And he that reaps receives wages, and gathers fruit unto life eternal: that both he that sows and he that reaps may rejoice together. And herein is that saying true, one sows, and another reaps.   *Jn. 4:36–37*

Neither as being lords over God's heritage, but being examples to the flock. And when the Chief Shepherd shall appear, you shall receive a crown of glory that fades not away.   *1 Pet. 5:3–4*

Promises to the Obedient

If you will diligently hearken to the voice of the Lord your God, and will do that which is right in his sight, and will give ear to his commandments, and keep all his statutes, I will put none of these diseases upon you, which I have brought upon the Egyptians, for I am the Lord that heals.   *Ex. 15:26*

Now therefore, if you will obey my voice indeed, and keep my covenant, then you shall be a peculiar treasure unto me above all people: for all the earth is mine.   *Ex. 19:5*

For I the Lord your God am a jealous God, visiting the iniquity of the fathers upon the children unto the third and fourth generation of them that hate me; and showing mercy unto thousands of them that love me, and keep my commandments.   *Ex. 20:5–6*

But if you shall indeed obey, and do all that I speak; then I will be an enemy unto your enemies, and an adversary unto your adversaries.   *Ex. 23:22*

And you shall serve the Lord your God, and he shall bless your bread, and your water; and I will take sickness away from your midst.   *Ex. 23:25*

You shall keep therefore his statutes, and his commandments, which I command you this day, that it may go well with you, and with your children after you, and that you may prolong your days upon the earth, which the Lord your God gives you, for ever.

Deut. 4:40

That you might fear the Lord your God, to keep all his statutes and his commandments, which I command you; you, and your son, and your son's son, all the days of your life; and that your days may be prolonged.

Deut. 6:2

Observe and hear all these words which I command you, that it may go well with you, and with your children after you for ever, when you do that which is good and right in the sight of the Lord your God.

Deut. 12:28

And it shall come to pass, if you shall hearken diligently unto the voice of the Lord your God, to observe and to do all his commandments which I command you this day, that the Lord your God will set you on high above all nations of the earth: and all these blessing shall come on you, and overtake you, if you shall hearken unto the voice of the Lord your God. Blessed shall you be in the city, and blessed shall you be in the field. Blessed shall be the fruit of your body, and the fruit of your ground, and the fruit of your cattle, the increase of your kin, and the flocks of your sheep. Blessed shall be your basket and your store. Blessed shall you be when you come in, and blessed shall you be when you go out.

Deut. 28:1–6

And if you will walk in my ways, to keep my statutes and my commandments, as your father David did walk, then I will lengthen your days.   *1 Ki. 3:14*

Blessed is the man that walks not in the counsel of the ungodly, nor stands in the way of sinners, nor sits in the seat of the scornful.   *Ps. 1:1*

All the paths of the Lord are mercy and truth unto such as keep his covenant and his testimonies.   *Ps. 25:10*

But the mercy of the Lord is from everlasting to everlasting upon them that fear him, and his righteousness unto children's children; to such as keep his covenant, and to those that remember his commandments to do them.

Ps. 103:17–18

Blessed are the undefiled in the way, who walk in the law of the Lord. Blessed are they that keep his testimonies, and that seek him with the whole heart.

Ps. 119:1–2

But whoso hearkens unto me shall dwell safely, and shall be quiet from fear of evil.
Pr. 1:33

If you are willing and obedient, you shall eat the good of the land.
Isa. 1:19

But this thing commanded I them, saying, Obey my voice, and I will be your God, and you shall be my people: and walk in all the ways that I have commanded you, that it may be well unto you.
Jer. 7:23

Yet you say, Why? Does not the son bear the iniquity of the father? When the son has done that which is lawful and right, and has kept all my statutes, and has done them, he shall surely live.
Ezek. 18:19

Whosoever therefore shall break one of these least commandments, and shall teach men so, he shall be called the least in the kingdom of heaven: but whosoever shall do and teach them, the same shall be called great in the kingdom of heaven.
Mt. 5:19

For whosoever shall do the will of my Father which is in heaven, the same is my brother, and sister, and mother.
Mt. 12:50

And he answered and said unto them, My mother and my brethren are these which hear the word of God, and do it.
Lu. 8:21

Blessed are they that hear the word of God, and keep it. **Lu. 11:28**

Verily, verily, I say unto you, If a man keep my saying, he shall never see death. **Jn. 8:51**

If any man serve me, let him follow me; and where I am, there shall also my servant be: if any man serve me, him will my Father honor. **Jn. 12:26**

He that has my commandments, and keeps them, he it is that loves me: and he that loves me shall be loved of my Father, and I will love him, and will manifest myself to him. **Jn. 14:21**

Jesus answered and said unto him, If a man love me, he will keep my words: and my Father will love him, and we will come unto him, and make our abode with him. **Jn. 14:23**

If you keep my commandments, you shall abide in my love; even as I have kept my Father's commandments, and abide in his love. **Jn. 15:10**

But whoso keeps his word, in him verily is the love of God perfected: hereby know we that we are in him. **1 Jn. 2:5**

And the world passes away, and the lust thereof: but he that does the will of God abides for ever. *1 Jn. 2:17*

And he that keeps his commandments dwells in him, and he in him. And hereby we know that he abides in us, by the Spirit which he has given us. *1 Jn. 3:24*

Promises to the Repentant

If they shall confess their iniquity, and the iniquity of their fathers, with their trespass which they trespassed against me, and that also they have walked contrary unto me; And that I also have walked into the land of their enemies; if then their uncircumcised hearts be humbled, and they then accept of the punishment of their iniquity: then will I remember my covenant with Jacob, and also my covenant with Isaac, and also my covenant with Abraham will I remember; and I will remember the land. *Lev. 26:40–42*

If my people, which are called by my name, shall humble themselves, and pray, and seek my face, and turn from their wicked ways; then will I hear from heaven, and will forgive their sin, and will heal their land. *2 Chr. 7:14*

For if you turn again unto the Lord, your brethren and your children shall find compassion before them that lead them captive, so that they shall come again into this land: for the Lord your God is gracious and merciful, and will not turn away his face from you, if you return unto him. *2 Chr. 30:9*

The Lord is nigh unto them that are of a broken heart; and saves such as be of a contrite spirit. *Ps. 34:18*

He heals the broken in heart, and binds up their wounds.   **Ps. 147:3**

Come now, and let us reason together, says the Lord: though your sins be as scarlet, they shall be as white as snow; though they be red like crimson, they shall be as wool.   **Isa. 1:18**

Let the wicked forsake his way, and the unrighteous man his thoughts: and let him return unto the Lord, and he will have mercy upon him; and to our God, for he will abundantly pardon.   **Isa. 55:7**

Promises to Those Who Reverence God

The angel of the Lord encamps round about them that fear him, and delivers them.
Ps. 34:7

For as the heaven is high above the earth, so great is his mercy toward them that fear him. As far as the east is from the west, so far has he removed our transgressions from us. Like as a father pities his children, so the Lord pities them that fear him.
Ps. 103:11-13

But the mercy of the Lord is from everlasting to everlasting upon them that fear him.
Ps. 103:17

Blessed is the man that fears the Lord, that delights greatly in his commandments.
Ps. 112:1

He will bless them that fear the Lord, both small and great.
Ps. 115:13

Blessed is every one that fears the Lord; that walks in his ways.
Ps. 128:1

He will fulfill the desire of them that fear him: he also will hear their cry, and will save them.
Ps. 145:19

The fear of the Lord prolongs days: but the years of the wicked shall be shortened.

Pr. 10:27

The fear of the Lord leads to life; and he who has it rests satisfied; he will not be visited by harm.

Pr. 19:23 RSV

It is good to grasp the one and not let go of the other. The man who fears God will avoid all extremes.

Ec. 7:18 NIV

Though a sinner do evil a hundred times, and his days be prolonged, yet surely I know that it shall be well with them that fear God, which fear before him.

Ec. 8:12

Promises to the Righteous

The righteous also shall hold on his way, and he that has clean hands shall be stronger and stronger.
Job 17:9

If they obey and serve him, they shall spend their days in prosperity, and their years in pleasures.
Job 36:11

Blessed is the man that walks not in the counsel of the ungodly, nor stands in the way of sinners, nor sits in the seat of the scornful. But his delight is in the law of the Lord; and in his law he does meditate day and night. And he shall be like a tree planted by the rivers of water, that brings forth his fruit in his season; his leaf also shall not wither; and whatsoever he does shall prosper.
Ps. 1:1–3

The angel of the Lord encamps round about them that fear him, and delivers them.
Ps. 34:7

The Lord redeems the soul of his servants: and none of them that trust in him shall be desolate.
Ps. 34:22

Delight yourself also in the Lord; and he shall give you the desires of your heart. Commit your way unto the Lord; trust also in him; and he shall bring it to pass.

Ps. 37:4–5

Cast your burden upon the Lord, and he shall sustain you: he shall never suffer the righteous to be moved.

Ps. 55:22

Blessed are the undefiled in the way, who walk in the law of the Lord.

Ps. 119:1

The Lord will perfect that which concerns me: your mercy, O Lord, endures for ever: forsake not the works of your own hands.

Ps. 138:8

The Lord preserves all them that love him: but all the wicked will he destroy.

Ps. 145:20

The Lord opens the eyes of the blind: the Lord raises them that are bowed down: the Lord loves the righteous.

Ps. 146:8

He that says unto the wicked, You are righteous; him shall the people curse, nations shall abhor him: but to them that rebuke him shall be delight, and a good blessing shall come upon them.

Pr. 24:24–25

Then shall your light break forth as the morning, and your health shall spring forth speedily: and your righteousness shall go before you; the glory of the Lord shall be your reward. *Isa. 58:8*

Blessed is the man that trusts in the Lord, and whose hope the Lord is. *Jer. 17:7*

Seek first the kingdom of God, and his righteousness; and all these things shall be added unto you. *Mt. 6:33*

And whosoever shall give to drink unto one of these little ones a cup of cold water, he shall in no wise lose his reward. *Mt. 10:42*

Love your enemies, and do good, and lend, hoping for nothing in return: and your reward shall be great, and you shall be the children of the Highest: for he is kind unto the unthankful and to the evil. *Lu. 6:35*

But as it is written, Eye has not seen, nor ear heard, neither have entered into the heart of man, the things which God has prepared for those that love him.
1 Cor. 2:9

Therefore let no man glory in men. For all things are yours; whether Paul, or Apollos, or Cephas, or the world, or life, or death, or things present, or things to come; all are yours. *1 Cor. 3:21–22*

And let us not be weary in well doing: for in due season we shall reap, if we faint not.

Gal. 6:9

And the peace of God, which passes all understanding, shall keep your hearts and minds through Christ Jesus.

Phil. 4:7

But the Lord is faithful, who shall establish you, and keep you from evil.

2 Th. 3:3

And he that overcomes, and keeps my works unto the end, to him will I give power over the nations.

Rev. 2:26

He that overcomes, the same shall be clothed in white raiment; and I will not blot out his name out of the book of life, but I will confess his name before my Father, and before his angels.

Rev. 3:5

Then I heard a voice from heaven say, Write: Blessed are the dead who die in the Lord from now on. Yes, says the Spirit, they will rest from their labor, for their deeds will follow them.

Rev. 14:13 NIV

Promises of the Future

Promises of Dwelling with Christ Forever

Promises of Eternal Life

Promises of Future Glory

Promises of Heavenly Reward

Promises of Inheritance

Promises of Resurrection

Promises of Seeing God

Promises of Precious Crowns

Promises of Dwelling with Christ Forever

[T]he righteous shall be in everlasting remembrance.

Ps. 112:6

[R]ejoice that your names are written in heaven.

Lu. 10:20 NIV

In my Father's house are many mansions: if it were not so, I would have told you. I go to prepare a place for you. And if I go and prepare a place for you, I will come again, and receive you unto myself; that where I am, there you may be also.

Jn. 14:2–3

Father, I want those you have given me to be with me where I am, and to see my glory, the glory you have given me because you loved me before the creation of the world.

Jn. 17:24 NIV

When Christ, who is our life, shall appear, then shall you also appear with him in glory.

Col. 3:4

Then we which are alive and remain shall be caught up together with them in the clouds, to meet the Lord in the air: and so shall we ever be with the Lord.

1 Th. 4:17

He died for us, that whether we wake or sleep, we should live together with Him.

1 Th. 5:10

Promises of Eternal Life

And many of them that sleep in the dust of the earth shall awake, some to everlasting life, and some to shame and everlasting contempt. And they that be wise shall shine as the brightness of the firmament; and they that turn many to righteousness as the stars for ever and ever. *Dan. 12:2–3*

And every one that has forsaken houses, or brothers, or sisters, or father, or mother, or wife, or children, or lands, for my name's sake, shall receive a hundredfold, and shall inherit everlasting life. *Mt. 19:29*

And these shall go away into everlasting punishment: but the righteous into life eternal. *Mt. 25:46*

That whosoever believes in him should not perish, but have eternal life. For God so loved the world, that he gave his only begotten Son, that whosoever believes in him should not perish, but have everlasting life. *Jn. 3:15–16*

He that believes on the Son has everlasting life: and he that believes not the Son shall not see life; but the wrath of God abides on him. *Jn. 3:36*

But whosoever drinks of the water that I shall give him shall never thirst; but the water that I shall give him shall be in him a well of water springing up into everlasting life.

Jn. 4:14

Verily, verily, I say unto you, he that hears my word, and believes on him that sent me, has everlasting life, and shall not come into condemnation; but is passed from death unto life.

Jn. 5:24

And this is the will of him that sent me, that every one which sees the Son, and believes on him, may have everlasting life: and I will raise him up at the last day.

Jn. 6:40

And I give unto them eternal life; and they shall never perish, neither shall any man pluck them out of my hand.

Jn. 10:28

He that loves his life shall lose it; and he that hates his life in this world shall keep it unto life eternal.

Jn. 12:25

As you have given him power over all flesh, that he should give eternal life to as many as you have given him.

Jn. 17:2

To them who by patient continuance in well-doing seek for glory and honor and immortality, eternal life.

Rom. 2:7

But now being made free from sin, and become servants to God, you have your fruit unto holiness, and the end everlasting life. For the wages of sin is death, but the gift of God is eternal life through Jesus Christ our Lord. *Rom. 6:22–23*

For he that sows to his flesh shall of the flesh reap corruption; but he that sows to the Spirit shall of the Spirit reap life everlasting. *Gal. 6:8*

But for that very reason I was shown mercy so that in me, the worst of sinners, Christ Jesus might display his unlimited patience as an example for those who would believe on him and receive eternal life. *1 Tim. 1:16 NIV*

In hope of eternal life, which God, that cannot lie, promised before the world began. *Titus 1:2*

And this is the promise that he has promised us, even eternal life. *1 Jn. 2:25*

These things have I written unto you that believe on the name of the Son of God; that you may know that you have eternal life, and that you may believe on the name of the Son of God. *1 Jn. 5:13*

And there shall be no night there; and they need no candle, neither light of the sun; for the Lord God gives them light: and they shall reign for ever and ever. *Rev. 22:5*

Promises of Future Glory

Then shall the righteous shine forth as the sun in the kingdom of their Father.
Mt. 13:43

For I reckon that the sufferings of this present time are not worthy to be compared with the glory which shall be revealed in us.
Rom. 8:18

When Christ, who is our life, shall appear, then shall you also appear with him in glory.
Col. 3:4

Therefore I endure all things for the elect's sakes, that they may also obtain the salvation which is in Christ Jesus with eternal glory.
2 Tim. 2:10

Who are kept by the power of God through faith unto salvation ready to be revealed in the last time.
1 Pet. 1:5

And when the Chief Shepherd shall appear, you shall receive a crown of glory that fades not away.
1 Pet. 5:4

Promises of Heavenly Reward

Rejoice, and be exceeding glad: for great is your reward in heaven. **Mt. 5:12**

Then shall the righteous shine forth as the sun in the kingdom of their Father.
Mt. 13:43

Then Jesus beholding him, loved him, and said unto him, One thing you lack: go your way, sell whatsoever you have, and give to the poor, and you shall have treasure in heaven: come, take up the cross and follow me. **Mk. 10:21**

When Jesus heard this, he said to him, You still lack one thing. Sell everything you have and give it to the poor, and you will have treasure in heaven. Then come, follow me. **Lu. 18:22 NIV**

Henceforth there is laid up for me a crown of righteousness, which the Lord, the righteous judge, shall give me at that day: and not to me only, but unto all them also that love his appearing. **2 Tim. 4:8**

Instead, they were longing for a better country—a heavenly one. Therefore God is not ashamed to be called their God, for he has prepared a city for them.
Heb. 11:16 NIV

Blessed is the man that endures temptations: for when he is tried, he shall receive the crown of life, which the Lord has promised to them that love him. *Jas. 1:12*

For so an entrance shall be ministered unto you abundantly into the everlasting kingdom of our Lord and Savior Jesus Christ. *2 Pet. 1:11*

Fear none of those things which you shall suffer: behold, the devil shall cast some of you into prison, that you may be tried; and you shall have tribulation ten days: be faithful unto death, and I will give you a crown of life. *Rev. 2:10*

And there shall be no night there; and they need no candle, neither light of the sun; for the Lord God gives them light: and they shall reign for ever and ever. *Rev. 22:5*

And, behold, I come quickly: and my reward is with me, to give every man according as his work shall be. *Rev. 22:12*

Blessed are they that do his commandments, that they may have right to the tree of life, and may enter in through the gates into the city. *Rev. 22:14*

Promises of Inheritance

Then shall the King say unto them on his right hand, Come, you blessed of my Father, inherit the kingdom prepared for you from the foundation of the world.

Mt. 25:34

And now, brethren, I commend you to God, and to the word of his grace, which is able to build you up, and to give you an inheritance among all them which are sanctified.

Ac. 20:32

To open their eyes, and to turn them from darkness to light, and from the power of Satan unto God, that they may receive forgiveness of sins, and inheritance among them which are sanctified by faith that is in me.

Ac. 26:18

Giving thanks unto the Father, who has qualified us to share the inheritance of the saints in light.

Col. 1:12 NASB

Knowing that of the Lord you shall receive the reward of inheritance: for you serve the Lord Christ.

Col. 3:24

That being justified by his grace, we should be made heirs according to the hope of eternal life.

Titus 3:7

Hearken, my beloved brethren, has not God chosen the poor of this world rich in faith, and heirs of the kingdom which he has promised to them that love him?

Jas. 2:5

To an inheritance incorruptible, and undefiled, and that fades not away, reserved in heaven for you.

1 Pet. 1:4

Promises of Resurrection

The hour is coming, in which all that are in the graves shall hear his voice, and shall come forth; they that have done good, unto the resurrection of life; and they that have done evil, unto the resurrection of damnation. *Jn. 5:28–29*

Knowing that he which raised up the Lord Jesus shall raise up us also by Jesus, and shall present us with you. *2 Cor. 4:14*

For the Lord himself shall descend from heaven with a shout, with the voice of the archangel, and with the trump of God: and the dead in Christ shall rise first. *1 Th. 4:16*

Promises of Seeing God

And after my skin has been destroyed, yet in my flesh I will see God.

Job 19:26 NIV

Blessed are the pure in heart: for they shall see God.

Mt. 5:8

Beloved, now are we the sons of God, and it does not yet appear what we shall be: but we know that, when he shall appear, we shall be like him; for we shall see him as he is.

1 Jn. 3:2

Promises of Precious Crowns

Everyone who competes in the games goes into strict training. They do it to get a crown that will not last; but we do it to get a crown that will last forever.

1 Cor. 9:25 NIV

Henceforth there is laid up for me a crown of righteousness, which the Lord, the righteous judge, shall give me at that day; and not to me only, but unto all them also that love his appearing.

2 Tim. 4:8

Blessed is the man that endures temptation: for when he is tried, he shall receive the crown of life, which the Lord has promised to them that love him.

Jas. 1:12

And when the Chief Shepherd shall appear, you shall receive a crown of glory that fades not away.

1 Pet. 5:4

Do not fear what you are about to suffer. Behold, the devil is about to throw some of you into prison, that you may be tested, and for ten days you will have tribulation. Be faithful unto death, and I will give you the crown of life.

Rev. 2:10 RSV

Personal Promises

Personal Promises

Scripture Abbreviations

OLD TESTAMENT

Gen.	Genesis	*Esth.*	Esther
Ex.	Exodus	*Job*	Job
Lev.	Leviticus	*Ps.*	Psalms
Num.	Numbers	*Pr.*	Proverbs
Deut.	Deuteronomy	*Ec.*	Ecclesiastes
Josh.	Joshua	*Song*	Song of Solomon
Judg.	Judges	*Isa.*	Isaiah
Ruth	Ruth	*Jer.*	Jeremiah
1 Sam.	1 Samuel	*Lam.*	Lamentations
2 Sam.	2 Samuel	*Ezek.*	Ezekiel
1 Kin.	1 Kings	*Dan.*	Daniel
2 Kin.	2 Kings	*Hos.*	Hosea
1 Chr.	1 Chronicles	*Joel*	Joel
2 Chr.	2 Chronicles	*Amos*	Amos
Ezr.	Ezra	*Obad.*	Obadiah
Neh.	Nehemiah	*Jon.*	Jonah

Mic.	Micah	*Hag.*	Haggai
Nah.	Nahum	*Zech.*	Zechariah
Hab.	Habakkuk	*Mal.*	Malachi
Zeph.	Zephaniah		

NEW TESTAMENT

Mt.	Matthew	*1 Tim.*	1 Timothy
Mk.	Mark	*2 Tim.*	2 Timothy
Lu.	Luke	*Titus*	Titus
Jn.	John	*Philem.*	Philemon
Ac.	The Acts	*Heb.*	Hebrews
Rom.	Romans	*Jas.*	James
1 Cor.	1 Corinthians	*1 Pet.*	1 Peter
2 Cor.	2 Corinthians	*2 Pet.*	2 Peter
Gal.	Galatians	*1 Jn.*	1 John
Eph.	Ephesians	*2 Jn.*	2 John
Phil.	Philippians	*3 Jn.*	3 John
Col.	Colossians	*Jude*	Jude
1 Th.	1 Thessalonians	*Rev.*	Revelation
2 Th.	2 Thessalonians		